# How Does Fruit Grow?

## FASCINATING FACTS ABOUT COMMON FRUITS

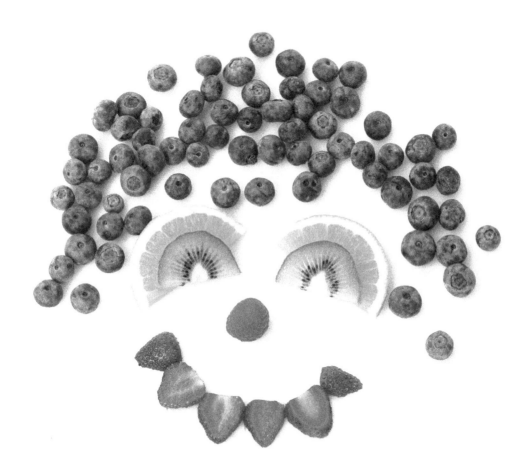

Written by Judy Roberts

Copyright 2020 by Judy Roberts

ISBN: 978-1-7354798-0-4

Cover and book design by Sue Balcer

# APPLE

Apples are eaten as fresh fruit and commonly used
to make juice, cider, applesauce and apple pie.

# Apples grow on trees.

A field of apples is called an orchard.

Apple trees bloom in the spring, set fruit, and take from 100 to 200 days to reach harvest in the fall.

## FUN FACTS

- The world's top apple producing countries are China, United States, Turkey and Poland.
- Apples are grown in all 50 states in the United States.
- There are over 7,500 varieties of apples.
- An apple tree can take at least 4 years to produce fruit then it can produce up to 500 apples each season.
- Apple trees grow to be up to 40 feet tall and live 50 to 80 years.

# APRICOT

Apricots are eaten as fresh fruit and commonly used to make jam, juice, dried apricots and desserts.

# Apricots grow on trees.

A field of apricots is called an orchard.

Apricot trees bloom in the spring, set fruit, and take from 100 to 120 days to reach harvest in the summer.

## FUN FACTS

The world's top apricot producing countries are Turkey, Iran, Uzbekistan and Algeria.

Apricots are grown on every continent except Antarctica.

There are about 12 common varieties of apricots.

An apricot tree can take at least 1 year to produce fruit then it can produce over 1000 apricots each season.

Apricot trees grow to be up to 30 feet tall and live 15 to 20 years.

# BANANA

Bananas are eaten primarily as fresh fruit and commonly used to make banana bread, pancakes, banana chips and desserts.

# Bananas grow on banana plants.

A field of bananas is called a plantation.

Banana plants take about 9 months to produce a flower then about 3 months for the bananas to ripen.

## FUN FACTS

- The world's top banana producing countries are India, China, Philippines and Ecuador.
- The banana is the most popular fruit. Over 100 billion are eaten around the world each year.
- There are over 1,000 varieties of bananas.
- An individual banana is called a finger. Each row of bananas is call a hand and is made up of 14 to 20 fingers. A single banana plant can produce up to 240 bananas
- A banana plant dies after the bananas are harvested but then new plants grow from the base for about 6 years.

# BLUEBERRY

Blueberries are eaten as fresh fruit and often frozen or dried. They are commonly used to make jam, muffins, pies and desserts.

# Blueberries grow on bushes.

Blueberries grow in fields and wild blueberries also grow on rocky hills called barrens.

Blueberries bloom in the spring, set fruit, and take about 90 days to reach harvest in the summer.

## FUN FACTS

- The world's top blueberry producing countries are United States, Canada, Turkey and Poland.
- Blueberries are one of the few fruit species native to North America.
- There are about 150 varieties of blueberries. There are 5 main types grown in the United States.
- A blueberry bush usually takes around 3 years to produce fruit then it can produce 800 blueberries each season.
- Blueberry bushes grow to be up to 12 feet tall and can live 50 years.

# CANTALOUPE

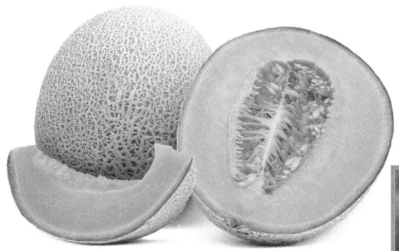

Cantaloupes are melons and they are
usually eaten as fresh fruit.

# Cantaloupes grow on plant vines.

Cantaloupes, a variety of muskmelons, grow in fields.

Cantaloupes bloom in late spring, set fruit, and take about 40 days to reach harvest in the summer.

## FUN FACTS

- The world's top cantaloupe producing countries are China, Turkey, Iran and India.

- In the United States, California is the leading producer of cantaloupes.

- There are 8 common varieties of cantaloupes.

- The melon is an annual plant.  It only produces fruit and lives for one season.

- The trailing cantaloupe vines can grow up to 9 feet in length.

# CHERRY

Cherries are primarily eaten as fresh fruit and commonly used to make cherry pie and dried cherries.

# Cherries grow on trees.

A field of cherry trees is called an orchard.

Cherry trees bloom in early spring, set fruit, and take from 55 to 90 days to reach harvest in the summer.

## FUN FACTS

- The world's top cherry producing countries are Turkey, United States, Russia and Ukraine.

- There are sweet cherries and sour cherries. There are around 1,200 varieties of cherries.

- A cherry tree takes at least 4 years to produce fruit then it can produce up to 7000 cherries each season.

- Cherry trees grow to be up to 25 feet tall and usually live about 25 years. There are three cherry trees in Japan over 1000 years old.

- Cherry trees are well known for their beautiful blossoms and cherry wood is often used to manufacture furniture.

# GRAPE

Grapes are eaten as fresh fruit and commonly used to make wine, grape juice, raisins and grape jelly.

# Grapes grow on plants called grapevines.

A field of grapevines is called a vineyard.

Grapevines bloom in the spring, set fruit, and take about
110 days to reach harvest in the fall.

## FUN FACTS

- The world's top grape producing countries are China, Italy, United States and France.
- There are around 8,000 varieties of grapes.
- A cluster of grapes is commonly known as a bunch of grapes. There are about 75 grapes in a bunch.
- A grapevine can take at least 3 years to produce fruit then it can produce up to 1,600 grapes each year.
- Grapevines can grow to be up to 50 feet long and live 50 to 100 years.

Kiwifruit are eaten as fresh fruit and commonly used
in baked goods and as a garnish.

# Kiwifruit grow on the vines of a plant.

Kiwifruit are grown in a field.

Kiwifruit vines flower in the early summer, set fruit, and take about 200 days to reach harvest in the late fall.

## FUN FACTS

- The world's top kiwifruit producing countries are China, Italy, Chile and New Zealand.

- There are about 50 varieties of kiwifruit.

- A kiwifruit plant can take at least 3 years to produce fruit then it can produce 600 kiwifruit each year.

- The woody vines of kiwifruit plants grow to be up to 40 feet long and the plants live about 40 years.

- Kiwifruit was originally called Chinese gooseberry then changed to kiwifruit, named after New Zealand's kiwi bird.

17

# MANGO

Mangoes are eaten as fresh fruit and commonly used
to make juice, smoothies, ice cream and salsa.

# Mangoes grow on trees.

A field of mango trees is called an orchard.

Mango trees bloom in the spring, set fruit, and take from 100 to 150 days to reach harvest in the summer.

## FUN FACTS

- The world's top mango producing countries are India, China, Thailand and Indonesia.
- There are over 400 varieties of mangos.
- A mango tree can take at least 3 years to produce fruit then it can produce around 300 mangoes each year.
- Mango trees grow to be up to 130 feet tall and can live 300 years.
- The mango is a tropical fruit growing best in climates with cool, dry winters and steamy, hot summers.

# ORANGE

Oranges are eaten as fresh fruit and commonly used to make juice, marmalade and zest from the peel.

# Oranges grow on trees.

A field of orange trees is called an orange grove.

Orange trees bloom in the spring, set fruit, and take from 7 months to a year to ripen.

## FUN FACTS

- The world's top orange producing countries are Brazil, China, United States and Mexico.
- Oranges are a citrus fruit and there are about 600 varieties.
- An orange tree can take at least 5 years to produce fruit then produces around 300 oranges each year.
- Orange trees grow to be about 30 feet tall and usually live about 50 years.
- Around 85% of all oranges produced are used for juice.

# PEACH

Peaches are usually eaten as fresh fruit and commonly used to make juice and desserts such as pie or ice cream.

# Peaches grow on trees.

A field of peaches is called an orchard.

Peach trees bloom in the spring, set fruit, and take from 90 to 150 days to reach harvest in the summer.

## FUN FACTS

- The world's top peach producing countries are China, Spain, Italy and Greece.
- There are over 2,000 varieties of peaches.
- A peach tree can take at least 2 years to produce fruit then it can produce around 500 peaches each season.
- Peach trees grow to be up to 30 feet tall and live about 12 years.
- Freestone peaches have fruit that easily pulls away from the pit, while clingstone flesh clings to the pit.

# PEAR

Pears are usually eaten as fresh fruit and canned, dried or used to make desserts.

# Pears grow on trees.

A field of pear trees is called an orchard.

Pear trees bloom in the spring, set fruit, and take from 115 to 165 days to reach harvest in early fall.

## FUN FACTS

- The world's top pear producing countries are China, Argentina, Italy and United States.
- There are about 3,000 varieties of pears.
- A pear tree can take at least 3 years to produce fruit then it can produce 300 pears each season.
- Pear trees grow to be up to 40 feet tall and can live up to 75 years.
- Pear wood is often used to construct musical instruments and furniture.

# PINEAPPLE

Pineapples are eaten as fresh fruit and commonly used to make juice, canned fruit, desserts and added to meat dishes.

# Pineapples grow on plants.

A field of pineapples is called a plantation.

Pineapple plants take at least 2 years to flower then about 6 months for the pineapple to ripen.

## FUN FACTS

- The world's top pineapple producing countries are Costa Rica, Philippines, Brazil and Thailand.

- There are 37 varieties of pineapples.

- A pineapple plant only flowers once and produces only 1 pineapple. But before it dies, new plants grow from the base and continue to produce pineapples for about 7 years.

- Pineapple plants usually grow to be 3 to 4 feet tall.

- A pineapple is a tropical fruit which is not a single fruit but actually a group of berries that have grown together.

# RASPBERRY

Raspberries are usually eaten as fresh fruit and commonly used to make jam and desserts or used as a garnish.

# Raspberries grow on the wood canes of plants.

Raspberry plants grow in fields.

Summer-bearing raspberry plants bloom in the spring and produce fruit in the summer. Everbearing raspberries produce fruit in the summer and again in the fall.

## FUN FACTS

- The world's top raspberry producing countries are Russia, Poland, United States and Serbia.

- There are over 50 varieties of raspberries.

- A raspberry plant usually takes about 2 years to produce fruit then it can produce more than 300 raspberries each season.

- Raspberry plants grow to be up to 7 feet tall and can live 20 years but their canes (branches) only live for 2 seasons.

- Each raspberry is made up of around 100 drupelets, each has juicy pulp and a seed. The berry is hollow on the inside.

# STRAWBERRY

Strawberries are eaten as fresh fruit and commonly used to make jam, drinks and desserts, often paired with cream or chocolate.

# Strawberries grow on plants.

Strawberry plants are grown in a field.

Strawberry plants bloom in the spring, set fruit, and take 30 to 40 days to ripen. Ever-bearing plants continue to flower and produce fruit through the summer.

## FUN FACTS

- The world's top strawberry producing countries are China, United States, Mexico and Spain.

- There are over 100 varieties of strawberries.

- A strawberry plant can produce fruit in the first year and it can produce up to 70 strawberries each season.

- Strawberry plants are usually up to 12 inches tall and produce runners that can be 8 to 18 inches long. They can live 5 to 6 years.

- There are about 200 seeds on an average strawberry.

# WATERMELON

Watermelon is usually eaten as fresh fruit and commonly used to make juice. The rind and seeds are also edible.

# Watermelons grow on the vines of plants.

Watermelons are grown in a field.

Watermelon vines bloom, set fruit, and take from 30 to 70 days
to reach harvest in the summer.

## FUN FACTS

- The world's top watermelon producing countries are China, Iran, Turkey and Brazil.

- There are more than 1,000 varieties of watermelons.

- A watermelon plant is an annual. The plant vines produce 2-4 watermelons and only live for 1 season.

- Watermelon plants grow to be up to 24 inches tall with vines that can grow 10 to 20 feet long.

- A watermelon usually contains 92% water. The average watermelon weighs about 20 pounds.

# Creative ways to eat fruit

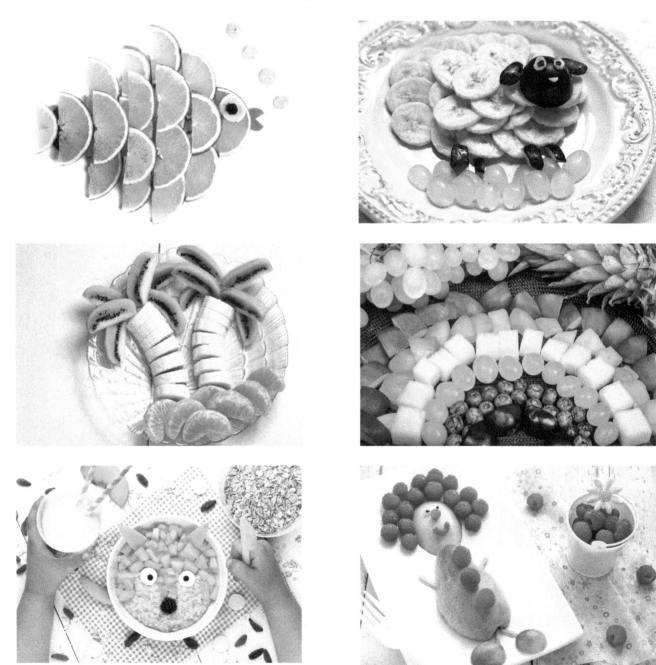

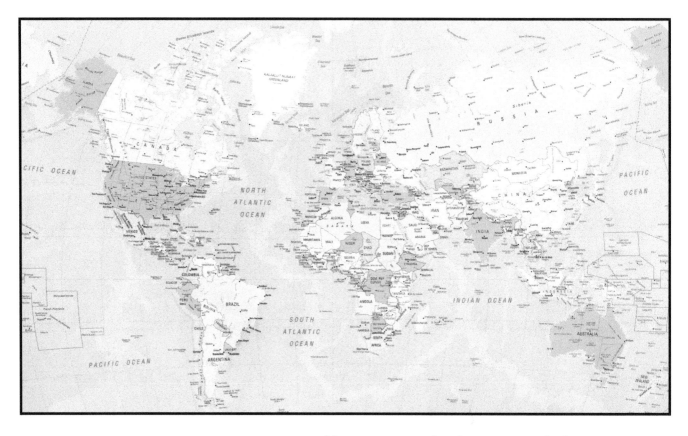

# Fruit is grown all around the world

**Apple**
China
United States
Turkey
Poland

**Blueberry**
United States
Canada
Turkey
Poland

**Grape**
China
Italy
United States
France

Orange
Brazil
China
United States
Mexico

Pineapple
Costa Rica
Philippines
Brazil
Thailand

Watermelon
China
Iran
Turkey
Brazil

Apricot
Turkey
Iran
Uzbekistan
Algeria

Cantaloupe
China
Turkey
Iran
India

Kiwifruit
China
Italy
Chile
New Zealand

**Peach**
China
Spain
Italy
Greece

**Raspberry**
Russia
Poland
United States
Serbia

Banana
India
China
Philippines
Ecuador

**Cherry**
Turkey
United States
Russia
Ukraine

Mango
India
China
Thailand
Indonesia

Pear
China
Argentina
Italy
United States

**Strawberry**
China
United States
Mexico
Spain

CPSIA information can be obtained
at www.ICGtesting.com
Printed in the USA
BVHW022257241120
593916BV00003BA/32